The Suicide's Wife
and Other Poems

Lucy Isabel Williams

Bleakswan Publications
Cambridge, Massachusetts

ISBN: 978-0-9962992-1-3 (sc)
ISBN: 978-0-9962992-0-6 (e)

Lulu Publishing Services rev. date: 7/2/2015

My husband took his own life on November 2, 1984. In remembrance, Jonathan Williams.

Lucy Isabel Williams was born in Evanston, Illinois in 1947 and has lived in Massachusetts for over forty years. She lives in Chestnut Hill, Massachusetts with her partner and near her children.

This is a book of writings, bits and pieces, about a life after a husband's suicide. Included are a few other poems. It was written over a period of 30 years.

For those who encouraged my writing:

all my friends, former writing group, especially Betsy Lowry and Bonnie Wax, Lee Rosenbaum, James Sabin, Mark Strand, reading group, Gale Barshop, Pamela Bauder, Ina Friedman, Stan Rauch, Jay Williams, Alex Jack, and my children, Molly Williams and Michael Williams.

Contents

Roses 1

Witnesses 2

Bone 3

After A Suicide Attempt 4

Incident 5

Funeral 6

Time 7

Suicide 8

What Was He Thinking 9

Morning 10

At the Grave 11

Defrosting 12

Blood 13

Moon 14

Lincoln Road 15

Dying Young 16

Falling 17

Poinsettia 18

Flowers from the Funeral 19

I Am a Virtual Funeral Parlor 20

The Sad Poems 21

Stonehenge 22

Widow 23

Sleep 24

Blue Moon 25
Hearse. 26
The Suicide's Wife 27
Thimble 31
Words 32
When Literature Comes. 33
You 34
Thanksgiving 35
Deed 36
No Good. 37
Mount Holyoke College 38
The Importance of Being Missed. .39
Life. 40
Fourth of July 41
Like a Bird 42
Writing. 43
Leaving Me 44
Tears 45
Moon 46
Pain. 47
Sadness. 48
My Book. 49

Roses

It was a night of sweet summer, how we remember summer,
Moon and darkness. We were celebrating something old,
Something we could not remember.

The four of us, and Jonathan and me.
We were sitting in his garden, my uncle's garden
Laughing at all things beautiful.
We were drinking. The air smelled like peaches,
But there were no peaches.
And then Jonathan came in from the dark,
Although I thought he was with us the whole time.
He came in with a vase of roses, roses that looked
Like pansies.
He presented them to me with a bow.
And then with a haunting grin, threw back his head
And drank all the water from the vase.
In that moment, I saw his destiny and the doom that would
Inflict the family.
That the beauty and the glitter of this family had no thing
To nourish it.
And those roses would be on our graves,
And especially for Jonathan, who would be the first.

Witnesses

When he died, everything was cut, put to scissors.
So what I write is bits and pieces.
The story of my life is cut so nothing can be too long.
Little sighs and moans of pain.
There can be no long novel because my story is over.
All I have are splinters that I pull out and hand to you,
Little witnesses.

Bone

I watched him die for years,
Down to the bone, to stone, so alone.
I don't know what he was thinking.
It could not have been good.

After A Suicide Attempt

I bring you oranges and put them at your feet.
I bring you raspberries to eat.
I put a pillow beneath your head.
I thank the dead.
I take away the knife,
I kiss your hair.
I preserve your life,
But your life is not there.

Incident

There was a small incident the day he died that
I remember. His mother gave me a gold locket with his picture
    in it. I knew immediately that she was giving me
This in place of something else. Something was missing,
There was an absence in this gift-and then I knew as if
My life was looking at me- that she had given the necklace to me
Instead of giving me his suicide note, a note never found. That
    she had kept it for herself had locked me out from him forever.
I wore the gold locket once,
But it felt like a little casket was around my neck and I hid it
    away.

Funeral

The day of the funeral there were a lot of people in the house.
People were dressing me and the children.
There was a feeling of frenzy and I thought I might be going
To the church to be married. The limo was black and shiny.
I waved to people out of the window.
I knew that I was important that day but I did not know why.
At the church my parents were meeting for the first time in
    thirteen years. I thought they might be getting married.
The minister said I was one of his favorite people and
He seemed pleased about something.
The coffin looked like the oak chest in my mother's bedroom
That she had borrowed from me the day she moved into the
    house.
I put roses on the coffin, flowers of blood.
There was singing and speaking. Then I walked down the aisle
    with
The minister to my black chariot to go to the next event.

Time

What do you think after all this time?
Of your death, your abandonment of us?
Does it feel right?

The past, present, future,
Swept away by your rope of death.
And little children bewildered by it.
How cruel you were. How cruel.
And so deep was your conviction to do us all in.

Suicide

When the sky fell in,
You were not at your desk writing to the stars.
You were not in the garden picking flowers for the moon.
You were not singing songs to the ravens at the river.
You were talking to that blackness, without me,
When the sky fell in.

What Was He Thinking

When you were dying,
You were thinking of me said the son,
How we would laugh at the world
Until I was stronger than you.
When you were dying,
You were thinking of me said the daughter,
You were planning stories to tell me
Into the night until I was a woman.
When you were dying,
You were thinking of me, said the wife.
How much was love when we were young,
How much was love.

Morning

She struggled through each night, almost as if it was death.
Fighting it, hating it.
And when it became light, she became calmer.
And the lightness of the morning sustained her.
Her room was like a little tomb.
The tomb was her life, her grave,
And she would get out of the grave each morning to live.

Getting into their bed was if it was a coffin.
She struggled with his death, his body each night.
Why did he die?
And the only comfort was morning,
For a few moments his death was gone.

At the Grave

It was a funeral by invitation only.
We invited flowers
Pink and blue.
They sat in their trenches, like soldiers,
Dying, never giving up
Like you.

Defrosting

After my mother heard that my husband had died, she decided
To defrost her refrigerator that night and brought over her frozen
    peas
To put into my refrigerator.
Years later friends would remark on this incident and how
    memorable it was,
Unsettling as everything else that happened that day.

Blood

I want to scratch your eyes out, like a cat.
Since you left me.
I want to lick your blood,
So I can be strong and walk away.

Moon

The lonely look the full moon gave me when you died
Was understandable.
Where can the moon find love
In a sky full of stars?
And where can I find the world where you are.

Lincoln Road

It came to me that I will end up here all my life, looking out of
the windows at my neighbors.
Please understand this is a bleak house, made from dreams and
deaths.
The black wreath, so old now, has blown off the door.
But that death is still around. When my husband died,
For one day I felt I would talk to him all day and work around
his death.
It was a terrible strain and I finally gave up the idea.

Dying Young

My blood is blue
From lack of oxygen, lack of you.
I feel faint, I drop to the ground.
I remember how you were,
Twenty years ago,
As time seeps into my bloody feet.
How you crossed the field,
Loving life in the strange way
That people do who will die young.

Falling

When my head hit the ice
I decided to keep going.
I would look for my husband
Who died years ago.
He would be young with happiness.
He would build a fire.
We would sit and sort out family secrets
And settle it once and for all
What was wrong in the family.
The fire would burn so brightly
That we could see the stars and moon above.
And the heat would make me
Rise to the surface,
Rise for both of us,
And the frozen petals of ice
Would make me look like a swan.

Poinsettia

Like a poinsettia
Hidden away all year, I bloom.
Is this a new year of grief?
How rich are the red blossoms
As they taunt the hope in me
For belief.

Flowers from the Funeral

I like cut flowers.
They wither with me.
Plants live.
I put myself in a glass vase each day and die.

I Am a Virtual Funeral Parlor

Come visit me, all of you who have lost too.
The dead greeting the dead is proper.
I will be kind.
But how to get out of this parlor
I cannot see.
Tell me how you did it, save my soul.
Come visit me.

The Sad Poems

The Sad Poems walk on stilts
To reach you in the sky.
Little meteors from my heart,
By and by.

Stonehenge

I wear Stonehenge on my head.
It looks antique, cool, mystifying, real.
It has become a big deal.
But the significance is actually low,
Just rocks and stones
That over the years broke my bones.

Widow

I have a wreath around my neck
That no one sees.
It is a consolation prize
For not being dead.
The pine scent makes it merry.
Keeping me upright and sound.
For everyday I live above the ground.

Sleep

I take my life off, like a dress
And go to sleep.

Blue Moon

I leave the window open
So the moon will come.
It is more faithful than you.
It comes every month in its white suit.
And with silver gloves holds me,
Like a beloved star.
I wake alone but know you will come back to me
Again and again,
Not leave me, like you did, in my life.

Hearse

Love goes quickly, like a dying friend.
I chase the hearse to make amends
The beloved laughs and condescends.
"Come back, come back" I pretend.
I race, I cry, I crash in the end.
The heart only learns at the final bend.

The Suicide's Wife

I insured my poem at Lloyds of London
It was pricey and the way was long.
But when I am old and love is gone,
I can go read it and remember
That it was for you.

Other Poems

Thimble

I was trying to find an image for my life,
That was small, compact, encompassing the littleness of my life,
Utilitarian.
And it came to me, a "thimble."
This image gave me solace, dignity.
And quite soon after that, I came across the image
In some one else's novel.
I was horrified, ashamed.
And for a long time I felt small, compact,
Perhaps like a thimble.

Words

Wipe the adverbs out of
My hair.
Words are tears
That no one reads.
They come without color.
They seek the well-read heart.

When Literature Comes

When Literature comes,
You will be there.
Words will hold hands like children,
And the perfect poem at the party
Will be placed in your lap.

You

I'll remember love
As I remember you.
The lover that never came,
Who climbed the tower
And fired at the crowd.

Thanksgiving

When I saw the kids bring up the cedar chest from my mother's
   home downstairs, I knew it meant something.
It was Thanksgiving, my mother's wedding anniversary.
There was something about the angle of the oak chest, coming
   up the crooked bleak stairs that set the tone for the rest of
   the day.
It was like my husband's coffin coming upstairs,
Home from the holidays, sent by my mother.

Deed

The deed has been done.
I have said good-bye to you.
I signed it, sealed, revealed it.
It is irrevocable and complete.
It is kind of neat,
To have it done.
Undone by one's own words.
But read between the lines
I am overcome.

No Good

Leaving breadcrumbs out
For you and the wolf
Did me no good.
I just had to go to the movies with him on Saturday
And put popcorn at his feet.

Mount Holyoke College

We live in jewelry boxes,
Amethyst and Secrets,
She smiled and said.
Then took her lumberjack to bed.

The Importance of Being Missed

The Importance of being missed,
The fact was not you.
You went across the sea
For a year to study, and you did.
And after all your talk of "people change,"
Missed me and came home.
But all those stamps,
Waves in my dreams,
I was waited out
By something other than you.
And when you did come home,
I was tired that night
And washed my gloves in the sink.
Waiting was perfection.
I did marry you, but it was not
The meaning of my life,
It was one of your letters,
Not you
Washed out, blurred by the sea in my red gripped garden.
The fact was not you.

Life

I searched the house for a word to describe my life.
It looked under pillows and into drawers I never opened before.
It will be a fine word,
Quite fine I tell my family.
They start hunting too.
I need this word to keep going.
People will understand when they hear this word.
They will know my life was something.
And that I did not waste it.

Fourth of July

The July of the heart knows no time.
Fireflies loom in my galaxy
Lighting up the past picnics,
Of sweetness and jubilee.
But the flag inside me withers
As I remember thee.

Like a Bird

I am like the bird
That is shot down
And becomes extinct.

Writing

I bite my fingers off
When I can not write.
They look like crayons,
From a child in therapy.

Leaving Me

After you left me, I took up
Sports, knitted afghans, sold soap.
Made jars of honey,
Sawed rope. Made baskets of peaches.
Quit school.
I guess hobbies is the general rule.

Tears

I lip-read softly your sallow eyes,
With all their truth and home-made lies.
And know you see me not at all.
And all the while, you did not dream of me.
I've just gone blind for several years,
Reading your tears as tears.

Moon

When I was five, I met the moon. I knew right away it was my
real mother.
It would come down from the sky and comfort me and I had to
grow up.
It had many moods and I understood when it would leave me
for days. And when it was as large as a white pancake in the
sky I would lie in its light to be healed.
That light made me grow up and I took on tasks in the world
and found my own family.
I left the moon behind. I did not have time. When my mother
on earth died, I felt sad. I wanted the moon to come back to
me. I would leave the window open at night. I felt sad that I
had not held my mother like the moon.
And the moon came for a while and held me as a child again.
Now I am old, too old for the moon. I am tired of the light that
heals. I don't want a mother any more. I need my father, my
real father, that black darkness of death.

Pain

Pain does not go away
It comes back like black ants
In the spring.
Organized, logical, and clean
It has its mission and gets its
Work done,
Before the summer's cruel fun.

Sadness

The pine tree looks at me.
Its beauty is stunning.
The whole world is beautiful.
It overwhelms with its perfection.
And I am not part of it.
I am a bird not sitting on the tree,
Not singing songs of Spring.

I sit in the swing, as years go by
Waiting it out for my heart to revive.
A blue butterfly comes to look me in the eye.
As I turn to the road for the hearse to arrive.

My Book

When I die
They will find a complete book inside me.
It will be full of all the things
I never said.
And as the bones stay still,
The pages of the book will scatter
Like butterflies on flowers.